IMAGINE ME OVER THE RAINBOW

TERRA WILSON

First Edition 2022

Cover art by Marine J.
Book production by MysticqueRose Publishing Services LLC

ISBN (Paperback): 978-1-7357-487-2-6
ISBN (ebook) 978-1-7357-487-3-3

Dedication

To my wonderful students and others with disabilities, who gave me the gift of laughter, forgiveness, tolerance, and so much more. To the incredible parents I've met on this journey; your kindness and appreciation are forever in my heart. To the remarkable teachers and guides. Thank you all.

To Wade and Symone, my precious children. You have made my heart smile so wide that my lips could not help but express it. You have shared me with so many without complaint. You two were the wind under my wings that pushed me to soar. Love you.

To Walter and Marine, my parents who taught me so much about life and to never give up on my dreams. I hope I've made you proud, Dad and Mom. Thank you.

Bravo to my husband, W. Wilson, for your love, support, suggestions, and first-round editing of this book. Thank you again, honey.

To all other family and friends, near and far, and Bruce; I will carry you in my heart always. We lived life to the fullest, and it was grand. Deborah Ellis, I heard you clearly and understand. Skylar W., Debra Duffy, Stella Crosby, Mel Edwards, Janice W., Bobbie Thompson, Phyllis Anderson, Paul Wilson, Olou Kay, Joetta Moore, 4 Ricks, Lydia, Leatrice, and Linda. To all of you, our journey through life has been something else. We have traveled through our teenage years to adulthood and beyond. Look at us now; fabulous! To all the great chefs in my life; your delightful cooking catapulted my taste buds into a heavenly deliciousness forever etched in my memory. All of you made me feel wonderful. Thank you for your warm hugs, love, kindness, and your laughter at life, which will embrace my heart forever. My dear friends, you are loved forever by me. We had real fun, didn't we?

3

To Michael E., who has been in the hot fire of the furnace, enduring much and surviving much on his way to maturity. You are a formidable person. Believe it.

To Mitchell E., who stands before us a man. Tall and handsome. We are proud of you. You have a great future ahead. Share that beautiful smile you inherited with the world. You have just begun.

To our youth everywhere. You will stumble, and you will fall. Mistakes you will make from time to time. Do not fret. Learn from them. Pick up the pieces, and start anew with a different attitude, understanding, and purpose.

Contents

Homage

Voices from the past.

'Imagine' could not have been written without giving reverence to the ancestors who gave their all for our right to live free. They endured unimaginable pain and suffering so that you and I could thrive. Because of them, we can put our pen to paper, our fingers to all modern technologies, and express our voices and opinions for acknowledgment. All of us matter and we are enough. Thank you, unforgettable heroes. We stand on the shoulders of giants. Their voices are blowing in the wind, turning the pages of history to reveal remarkable people showing their true worth. Hear their voices in the trees as the wind blows, shaking the branches, whispering to you and me of love and peace: "Do not let history repeat itself. We are with you, our seeds that will plant generations to come. Love one another. Do not lose your way. Keep your eyes on the prize: life, liberty, and the pursuit of happiness — living in our beautiful world without fear, catapulted into a new day of peace."

We will speak their names and remember them through tears of empathy.

Introduction

The inspiration for this book of poems was pulled from my direct interactions and work with students and adults with disabilities. 'Imagine' poems represent the students' love for everyday living that they communicated to me, and the years dedicated to providing assistance and support to disabled students and helping adults reach their full potential in living their best lives. Our fellow travelers need a little help navigating their journey through life. They gave so much love and appreciation, and my love was returned double. People with disabilities are very trusting. Let us all advocate for them. They made me smile every day with their curiosity about life. I would spend hours answering questions about everyday occurrences. And I mean everything -- from 'how's' to 'why's' and 'what's.' All of this went into the computer of my brain. At the end of each day, my feelings would overwhelm me to write about their struggles. My desire is for people to feel and know the beauty people with disabilities have inside and out. They are in a world that is not of their making. Yet, they smile.

Human kindness is a touch of friendliness. It is my deepest hope that this book of poems will bring happiness to students and others, touch a heart somewhere, and lead to reflection on what is important in this life.

'Imagine' is about kindness, tolerance, empathy, understanding, and patience. How we treat our most vulnerable.

There is medical evidence indicating that our environment has poisons floating around in it. Children are going to be born with birth defects that lead to disabilities early and later in life due to genetics, hereditary characteristics, DNA, or severe trauma. We run the greatest risk for the greatest joy in life: our children. It is not anyone's fault when something goes wrong in nature that we do not expect or understand. Life happens. Birth defects do, too. We will take care of our children.

They are a part of us. All people of the universe are born with the same needs, including the desire to feel and know love. Our goal is to live our lives in happiness and peace and be treated with dignity and respect.

Disabled persons are afraid on this world stage they are on. They are afraid of being misused and abused.

They have difficulty communicating and comprehending the actions of others. Look into their eyes, and you'll see their fear of being misunderstood. Disabled people can perform just as well as others can. Developmental disabilities in children and adults range from mild to severe. But give them a little time, and they will do it. I am in awe of what they can do. It is truly delightful to have witnessed this and can now give a firsthand account of the students in action mastering their activities.

My eyes tear up and overflow as students and adults perform. Singing is one of the activities they love. The sound of them singing is as lovely as the sound of precious magical voices in a grand and beautiful opera. "When we sing, we feel free," the students informed us. "Through music, we touch people."

My wish is that you are thoroughly educated and armed with exact information about people with disabilities. I wish to awaken you to their inner beauty and their spirit to flourish. It is my hope that the stories of these students will warm your heart. Journey through my eyes, and you will smile and understand. Can you imagine that?

"She walked into the classroom and was greeted by silence and looks of apprehension. She smiled and said hello. The students smiled back and greeted her with shy hellos."

This is how my journey began with students and adults with special needs. They are in a world of uncertainty and find it difficult to express their needs or what they are feeling. These 'Imagine' poems, I hope, will shed light on the feelings the students have expressed to me.

These poems are meant for all who are physically, mentally, and psychologically handicapped, and for a world that is slowly opening up to them.

Inspiration for my first poem came from the memory of seeing how the nurses wrap babies in the hospital.

COCOON

Squirm, squirm.

Something holds me in.

What is this?

Scream, scream.

What trick is this?

I want to get out.

Please do not hold me in.

I squirm and I squirm to be free.

I hear, I feel, I smell.

Oh! How I squirm and

Squirm to be free.

Oh! How I squirm.

To be free.

14

HOLD MY HAND

People are holding hands as I watch from my window.

Couples are holding hands as they walk through the park.

It looks like so much fun.

A cool breeze blows.

At the touch of it, I shiver.

My hands reach out.

"Someone, please take my hand?"

I can't hold back.

Surrounded by light, darkness leaves.

Bitter tears, I shed.

Cascading down my face.

Displaying the pain.

In my heart of hearts, I cry.

Please, someone take my hand.

I wait.

OVER THE RAINBOW

Over the rainbow,

we can walk. We can run.

We can jump and skip.

There is happiness beyond your imagination.

Nothing is impossible.

Every dream will come true.

If you believe, you believe.

I can tell scary stories.

They will make you shiver with fright.

Over the rainbow,

we dance and dance.

We will swing high to the sky

and sing beautiful songs like birds.

It is said to be

that you can sail away into the sunset

toward unknown adventures

over the rainbow.

You can slay dragons and rescue princesses.

Someday, we will go there, if only in our dreams.

It all lays over the rainbow.

MOMMA

Where are you, Momma?

I am looking for you.

Momma, I want to talk to you.

Why do you not answer?

Momma, I miss you always.

Reaching out in the darkness

to touch you would be divine.

Walking alone with you,

planting a sweet kiss on your cheek

to feel your softness remembered.

Where are you?

I look for you in the face

of every stranger passing by.

The question still on the tip of my lips.

"Why did you leave me lonely?"

Love you still, Momma.

My Momma.

BANG, BANG

I do not mean to bang my head.

Bang, bang.

I do not mean to drool all the time.

Bang, bang.

Maybe if I bang hard enough,

it will stop.

Bang, bang.

Behind the Eyes

I have hopes and dreams

filled with love and trust.

Feelings, with needs like yours.

Am I someone like you?

When looking into your eyes,

I know I am not.

My soul thrives to be free.

Captured by fear, caged by inability.

Trapped with an uncertainty of life.

Remember, the eyes do not lie.

Now, look into my eyes and see.

LET ME SEE!

To see life as it

is in the daylight.

I can, you know.

No, no. Do not shut me in.

Please, no darkness today.

The night will arrive soon enough.

I can rest in it,

but cannot hide in it.

Do not abide in it.

Peace eludes me.

Why not surround me with the warmth of protection
that I want?

No perfection needed.

Where is the sweet touch of compassion?

Why is there darkness in daylight?

Night will surely come, as always.

Survive in it, I shall.

If I must.

A. E. I. O. U.

Oh me, oh my.

I can say it.

I heard it somewhere.

If only I knew what it means.

I do not care.

I am happy.

A.E.I.O.U.

TAP

Tap, tap.

My legs go tap, tap.

My hands go clap, clap.

In my head, I feel the fluidity of both.

Without connection.

If only I could move.

THINKING OF TEXAS

Texas white pellets of ice.

Green hills and valleys cover.

Slips and falls.

SKIERS AWAIT

Skiers stare hopefully

toward mountain tops,

waiting eagerly for snow.

THE POOL

Hmm mm, hmm mm.

How nice.

So soft, so cozy, so warm.

What is this?

Hmm mm, hmm mm.

I feel safe. I feel free.

My arms and legs sway ever so gently.

They can move.

Hmm mm, hmm mm.

Such peace and calm in this place.

Can I dare to close my eyes and sleep?

Hmm mm, hmm mm.

Where am I?

Is it Mother's womb?

Or just a sweet, sweet dream?

Please do not wake me.

THE DREAM

I hear the patter of little feet.

I hear a baby's laughter.

I hear a sweet voice saying,

"Honey, we are home."

Suddenly, my eyes open. I am alone.

All I hear is silence.

I HAD A DREAM

People speak of global warming.

The is Earth undergoing rapid change.

Nature is unable to cope.

We ignore one simple truth;

Only man holds the blame.

I had a dream.

One day, we shall be crying.

How all life, we are denying.

Repeating history once more.

Disappearing like dinosaurs.

I had a dream.

No clouds were in the sky.

Humanity was praying for rain each day.

"Pour your blessing down upon us.

We wait."

Words of Wisdom

*When shall you help a man?

When he is up or down?

*I am my brother's keeper.

*Love thy neighbor as you

love yourself.

*Blessed is the peacemaker.

*Beware of wolves (people) in sheep's clothing.

Presenting themselves as one thing when, really, they are something else.

Different from the character they show up as.

*Do not venture into places you are not familiar with (places you do not know).

*Love yourself, then love someone else.

*Just when you think it is all over,

your world can change in an instant.

You do not know what is around the corner.

Do not give up.

*Even though your heart is breaking, smile.

*Stop, and smell the roses of life.

*Do unto others as you would have them do unto you.

*Be kind to every living thing.

*Take pleasure in all things. Enjoy what you have.

*Remember, you are loved by the universe.

* All that is here is good.

CRUSH

Got a crush on you.
What a feeling of
anticipation,
breathlessness!
You envelop my senses
intensely.
Like smoke-filled
lungs that gasp for air,
you hold tight my throat.
As the grip of a turtleneck sweater.
Unable to breathe.
To say something.
Anything.
Got a crush on you.
I cannot speak.

THE TOP

Never-ending climb.

They loom in front of me.

Where do the stairs end?

One, two, three, on they go.

Can I make it there?

To Neverland?

Wow! It is me.

I will do it.

Watch and be amazed.

The climb is long and weary.

Keep climbing and striving.

The top is in sight.

Succeed. Yes, I must do it.

No tumbling.

Do not look down.

Keep looking up.

Keep climbing. You are there.

Welcome to accomplishment land.

Landing at the top of the stairs.

Well done!

YOU

A gift from the universe.

"You."

You are our love.

You are our daily bread.

You are the sunshine of our life.

You are the taste of honey in this
sometimes sour world.

You are one of the beautiful flowers
in my humble garden.

You inspire me to be my best.

You are the peace in my heart.

Your hugs and kisses are truth.

Honest, so warm, so real, so pure.

You are my spring in winter.

You are the light in the darkness.

You do not know it, but you give us hope.

"Yes, you."

ANGELS

Angels I call upon to help guide and counsel me
through this land of uncertainty and strife.
Yet, there is evil here, too!
Perhaps there is, perhaps not.

ANGEL WINGS

When the angels see the
pain that lives inside of me,
always, they will come and
wrap their wings around me.
Now, there is no more pain
I'm free.

I SEE YOU

I feel your heart.

Acceptance is what you crave.

Look at your strength,

not your weakness.

You may not be tidy.

There is confusion in your eyes.

You want to do the right thing.

You want to learn.

I see you.

You need to give love.

You have dreams and aspirations.

The future is out there.

You are seeking the answer

to the questions, "Why am I here?"

"Where is my place in this life?"

"Can someone tell me please?"

Lost, you are.

Do not despair.

I see you.

LIGHT

You are the sunshine in my darkest hour.

It is you that helps heal the brokenhearted.

Pieces once scattered, now together again.

BRAVERY

In the midst of the storm,

you lifted me up when I could no longer stand.

You were the wind under my wings.

You did not falter.

You. A lion, as fierce as you are beautiful.

Casting a giant shadow, taking control of a chaotic situation.

Completely engaged. Action.

A brave soldier on the field of battle.

Your true character emerging,

going beyond the call of duty.

You, thinking only of the welfare of others,

not yourself or the cost.

I salute you.

I AM A MAN

Men walk the talk
and stand for what's right.

A man protects.

A man is kind.

A man is upright.

A man is good.

A man is gentle.

A man is strong.

A man sheds tears,

sometimes at night.

A man tries to understand.

Looks into your eyes.

Takes your hand.

Makes you feel that everything is alright.

Look at me.

I am a man.

JUST CALL ME SWEETIE

Somebody, will you call me 'Sweetie', please?

I've heard someone say it before.

It sounded so good.

Hungry for words of affection.

For my ears only.

"Sweetie."

Somewhere, I will hear them.

Is it too much to ask?

It is not too much to ask for in this life.

It is ringing in my head. "Sweetie."

It is there when I go to bed. "Sweetie."

The thought of it makes my face red.

The feeling is from head to toe.

"Sweetie."

Those words toss around gently in my head.

Thinking of you as

my friend, my confidant.

"Sweetie."

"Am I awake or dreaming?"

Taking your hand, hoping to hear

you say, "Sweetie."

I smile at you.

Look into my eyes, dancing in

anticipation.

"Say it, please."

What is so wrong with this small request?

To hear those words

meant just for me.

"Sweetie."

I FEEL

My heart beats fast.

My mind is fuzzy.

My stomach flutters.

You think I do not feel love

because of what you do.

I feel love.

I embrace love.

I am safe within,

touched and touching.

I want to feel good all over.

It would be so wonderful.

Be happy for me.

Rejoice in my happiness.

I feel love, I feel love.

CALL OF THE WILD

Trapped. My body is yearning,

spurred by the howling of nature.

A universal need

driving all creatures.

A call of the wild

leaving desires unanswered.

I am not sure what it is.

All I know is that I feel something

surging through me.

"Is it the call of the wild?"

OR

"Another seizure?"

THE CIRCLE

Your circle of arms
feels so good.
Like a warm blanket on my bed
or my favorite coat surrounding me in winter.
Why hasn't anyone done this before?
I do not want to leave
this circle of warmth.
It feels safe and protected.
It feels so familiar.
I do not remember.
Try and remember; I do not.
"Hug me again sometime."
I like familiar.

THE HUG

Hug you. Yes.

You are too far away.

Can I hug you?

Or will you walk away?

READY FOR LOVE

Love can raise you up so high.

Love can pull you down so low.

One thing I know.

Love will always show

up for me.

Ready when love

shows up for me.

SURRENDER

I am so pale, so frail.

I am so weak.

Unable to speak.

So cold, I've lost my heat.

It takes all of me to sit here.

I am among the meek who have

to surrender to others.

You say I do not smile at you.

You say I do not speak when spoken to.

"Do you want to hear me squeak?"

You say I am rude. No, darling.

I want to talk. I want to smile big.

Today, my illness has a strong grip on me.

I try and fight it, but

I am barely making it today.

Let me feel the warmth of your smile.

Let me hear the joy in your voice.

Let your spirit lift me up. Give me a hug.

Do not judge me wrong.

Today, I am barely making it.

"I surrender."

OH! JOHNNY BOY

Johnny boy, oh, Johnny boy.

Why are you crying?

Beauty is all around,

made by you.

No. You do not see me.

No one hears me. I cannot speak.

I stamp my feet to get attention.

I even cry.

No, not bad as you say.

Just sad, trying to be good.

Am I quiet enough?

I do not need much.

Take care of me; that's all I want.

Look into my eyes, I am here.

Dream, dream is all I can do about one day how

I will triumph and take care of me.

But 'til then, you understand."

Today, Johnny boy needs your help.

BAR-B-QUE

Hmm mm, hmm mm.
I can smell it, taste it.
Smoke enters my nose.
It is so delightful.
Aroma has aroused
my taste buds for all that there is to eat.
Delicious potato salad, baked beans.
Punch, lemonade, cake, and so many
other delicious treats.
Wow! I can taste it now.
My mouth starts to water in
anticipation, thinking of it.
"Oh! How I love bar-b-que."
Summer is in the air.
The sun is out in front of a blue sky.
It is so beautiful. The day is perfect.
Birds are singing and chirping.
Bees are buzzing around.
Trees are moving back and forth.
Dancing with delight as the wind blows.
Everyone is happy. I cannot wait. I love bar-b-que.
My excitement is too much.
"Bar-b-que!"
Only I wasn't invited.

THE SCREAM

Take me out to the ball game.

Take me out so I can scream.

Scream as loud as I can.

Can anyone hear me?

Anyone?

EYES

What is it that you want to see?

Do you really look? Or just gaze?

I wonder, "Can you ever concentrate?"

Tell me truthfully.

Do you want your eyes to be clear?

DAFFODILS

Waiting.

Eager for spring.

Yellow daffodils bloom

in the late winter months.

TICK TOCK, TICK TOCK

Oh me, oh my.

There it goes again.

My body calls.

It grabs me like a soft fall.

My stomach tightens.

Feeling frightened.

It is so lonely here in the dark.

Tick tock, tick tock,

Goes the clock on the wall.

The sound enters my head.

Stop! Please stop.

It goes on and on.

Tick tock, tick tock.

Hopefully, by morning it will

have gone away. Now, I sleep.

Precious sleep. As the clock

on the wall goes...

tick tock, tick tock.

THE DANCE

In the darkness, under the warm cloak of

my soft cotton blanket that wraps around

my body, imitating the effect of a cocoon.

How safe it feels, how serene.

Drifting into another world.

I hear, "Let my arms encircle you.

Come dance with me here under the moonlight.

Let our feet take flight."

Spinning, twirling.

Oh! To be free, so free.

We are dancing on a cloud in space,

among the stars.

This is where I belong. My reality.

Light as a feather.

Anything is possible.

Please. Do not wake me.

No! Not yet.

Let me finish dancing.

This dream may never come again.

Dance, little feet, dance.

SUNSHINE

It is warm. It is hot.

"What is this that

reaches out and lights up my face?"

Glow is now on my hands.

Warmth touches my chest.

Oh! Beautiful glow, that circle.

Like the arms of a good friend.

Like a mother's hug.

A warm glass of milk on a chilly night traveling down

my neck cavity to warm my stomach.

And flowing through the length of my body.

It feels so good. I smile all over.

Take me outside again soon to

feel the power of the sun.

RAYS

I know I am in the rays
of your sunshine.
It makes me feel good.
Smile again, and let me be the
beneficiary of your kindness.
The warmth of your rays
are in my heart
forevermore.

THIRST

My lips are dry.
My throat is dry.
My tongue hangs out of my mouth.
Can you not see me waving
my hand for your help?
It is impossible for me to reach up.
I cry and cry.
Oh me, oh my.
Now my eyes are dry.

WALKING

I feel like walking.
I want to walk.
My mind is saying, "walk."
If only my feet could hear me.
I'm telling my right foot, and
I'm telling my left foot to
"Move, move."

WINGS

You are the wind beneath my wings.
You carry me, and I know the
joy of each step.
"Are you an angel?"

LOOKS AND STARES

Your eyes are on me.

Your whispers I hear.

You look away.

Why do you walk away?

"It's okay.

I am here to stay."

Come on over, and say hey.

LIKE

I smile, I laugh.

I get hurt.

I like ice cream and cookies.

I like fried chicken and macaroni.

I like, love hamburgers and french fries.

I like walks in the park.

I like, love to play.

I like to go to concerts.

I like, love, love music.

I like, love television.

I like pretty clothes.

I like girls. I like boys.

I am like you.

Wow! I am you.

#SMILE

You make my heart smile. It travels to my lips.
Feeling the essence of your love through the
beautiful curves of your lips that you so elegantly
display.

YOU

I am thankful for you.
I need to go.
So many things to do.
Just think,
it is all for you.

CONTENTMENT

Sweet, quiet moments.
Baby boy and girl sleep in peace.
Mom's garden blossoms.

SPOIL

What does that imply?

What does that mean?

Yes, you say I am spoiled.

Can you not feel my desperation?

I cannot walk or talk,

only squeak.

No potty without assistance.

Cannot feed myself without assistance.

Spoiled, so spoiled.

My head moves up and down slowly.

Spoiled, so spoiled.

My eyes roll back in my head.

Spoiled, so spoiled.

You can move. I cannot.

Spoil me, please.

Let's trade places for a minute.

Imagine you were me.

ATTITUDE

"Attitude?" No!

Fortitude is what I have.

Tenacity is what I have.

Power is what I have.

Patience, tolerance is what I have.

Listening to, "do this, do that."

"You are bad today."

"Attitude today?" What?

I am here by grace.

I want to be good.

I just want to do something different today.

A choice is available, right?

Listen, please.

Do not have attitude today.

Is there no understanding?

Is there no empathy for me?

"Attitude?" No!

Just another day

And I am trying to get through it.

FEELINGS

"Hearing your voice is music to me
when you give out
praise."

BE GENTLE

Feeling funny, feeling strange.
I just feel different today.
Feeling confused or flippant?
I don't know.
Be gentle with me today.
I want to cry.
Need to cover my head and
just stay in bed.
Seeing red.
Be gentle with me today.
Do not know what is wrong.
Could be something they call
hormones.
Be gentle.
Yes. Be gentle with me today.
Thank you.

GREEN EYES

Emeralds, precious stones.

Bright and beautiful as

God's landscape.

Green eyes, green eyes.

Color so pure. Glowing. Shining.

I cannot tell as you stare with your green eyes.

What do you see?

THE SWING

Swing low, swing high.

I believe I can fly.

Swing low, swing high.

I see the sky.

Oh! It is so blue.

If you only knew

how it makes me feel.

I do not want to stop.

Swing low, swing high.

I can reach the top of the trees

until I touch the sky.

Push me, push me!

HEART BEATING

How wonderful,

how beautiful.

Let me hear your heart.

There is something about the beat.

It is so familiar.

It makes us one.

Pump, pump.

Now, breathe.

DON'T TOUCH ME

Show that you are something to see.

Walking in your name-brand

clothes with designer tags.

Walking with so much pride.

Assured in your stride.

"Don't touch me!"

Hardhearted.

Hands reaching out.

"Don't touch me!"

Watch where you step.

Do not stumble.

Do not fall.

BLUE EYES

Blue eyes, blue eyes.

Pools of ocean water.

Rare gems of beauty.

Trusting of the world.

Shimmering as the slow, calm

movement of a lake.

Speaking through

those eyes of blue,

Can you see me?

Sparkling, sparkling.

Looking at me.

SHAKES AND SHIVERS

Rain, rain, go away.

No thunder today.

No lights out today.

Let me stay on my feet.

Rain, rain, go away.

No shakes and shivers today.

POSSESSION

Oh no!

It grips me hard.

Un-fore-seen.

Forcefully.

It tosses me about

like a rag doll.

It shakes and sways me.

I am helpless.

I can do nothing.

Incapacitated.

I am at its mercy.

Down, down I go.

UNCERTAINTY

You reach for me. I pull away.

Oh! You wanted to kiss my cheek.

That is new.

TEARS

Water is running down my face.

I do not know why. It is salty.

"Stop, stop!"

It keeps running, and I do not know why.

My face feels hot to touch.

My eyes are full of water again.

It keeps running, and I do not know why.

Do you?

BOUNCE

Over here in this corner,

trying not to get in the way.

I want so desperately to play.

Bounce

My hands start to move, I feel it.

"You do not know how to play", you say.

"Let me pretend to play."

Bounce

"Throw me the ball."

Please tell me first.

Bounce

MY SONG

Hey! Wait a minute.

"That's my song!"

Arms start shaking.

Legs moving a little.

Eyes sparkling bright.

Moving side to side.

"That's my song!"

Feel that beat.

"Meet me on the dance floor."

"Groove with me."

Wow! I feel good.

"Come on."

"That's my song!"

A CHANCE

Come my way.

Tell them, show them.

To surround me is to drown me.

Let me move, let me groove.

"Give me a chance?"

A chance to prance.

A chance to dance.

For a moment,

just step away.

THE SMILE

Tall and handsome.

"Wow! So fine!"

You wave at me.

I wave back.

You smile at me.

I smile back.

You walk with pride.

A little pep in your stride.

You walk over to me and say hello.

Unable to speak.

Please, do not walk away.

"Stay."

TOUCH

Wow!

What is this?

It feels soft. It feels warm.

Feeling the texture of skin.

A smile appears on my face.

My body feels good all over.

It goes away very quickly.

"Please take my hand again."

HOME

Wishing for a place they call home.

Not a pretend one, a real home.

A place of love, peace, and shelter.

A place filled with hugs and kisses.

A place to feel safe from the world.

It can be very cold sometimes.

A place of warmth to rest at

the end of the day.

A place where open arms await me.

A place to fill my tummy. No more

hunger pangs. Delicious food.

A place with mother's smile and

gentle hands to soothe my broken

spirit. A mother's voice that is music.

A place with father's strong voice and

his big hugs.

To dream of a place called home.

I wait.

WHY?

I love you, and I do not know

why you do not love me.

And I do not know why.

I love you, and I know why.

People with disabilities come in all shapes, sizes, and colors. It does not discriminate; people come from everywhere in life. They could be you. They could be me. Always remember that you could walk in their shoes. Wear them for a while, and know what they go through every day. There is no time off for them. It could be me or you.

You never know. You just never know. BELIEVE IN RANDOM ACTS OF KINDNESS.

COVER ME

Please cover me.

Cover me with a warm blanket.

Cover me with a beautiful shawl.

Any soft cover will do.

My body twisted.

Cover me, please.

Then, I will look like you.

THE THRONE

Twists and turns.

Moans and groans.

Crying, trying.

Pushing, pushing.

Being on the throne

can be hell sometimes.

I yell.

I think.

Release.

RED, WHITE, AND BLUE

Red, white, and blue.

Home of the brave.

Not me today, babe.

I want to stay home.

Left alone.

Feeling so red and blue.

Forced to face the world.

Feeling mostly blue.

"Boohoo?"

Want to be in my bed,

snug as a bug in a rug.

Feeling this way.

If I may, but you do not hear me.

You wheel me out into the bright

sunlight.

Feeling so red and blue.

"Boohoo?"

PAIN

Fragile as a sparrow am I.

Can you hear me?

My knees are wounded.

"Please, can I ease into this seat?"

I need a minute,

a moment to be at peace.

Nature, release me from

pain.

WHAT COLOR IS GRAY?

What color is gray?

A cold and rainy day.

Drops of water on my face to

cover the tears.

RAIN BOOTS

Wow! New rain boots.

Yellow, green, red, purple.

All the colors of the rainbow.

Wee! Splash, splash.

What fun playing in the rain is.

"Wee, wee!" as I fall to the ground.

These shoes are too big.

On the wrong foot.

LITTLE HANDS

Little hands reach out.

Little hands hold mine.

Little hands try to touch my face.

Little hands clap with joy.

Little hands play patty cake.

Little hands try and feed themselves.

Phenomenal and delightful.

"You did it."

Mixed Messages

"Is this joy or pain?"

Do not know which.

"Is this good or bad?"

Should I be glad?

Should I be mad?

Should I cry?

Should I smile or jump for joy

As you hold my hand?

Do not know which.

Confused, not amused.

There is a twist.

"Is this love?"

WHY CAN'T I?

Why, oh, why

Can I not reach her?

Can I not give her a peach?

We could go to the beach.

I see her, she sees me.

Why can't I dance with her?

Why can't I stroll over to her?

I want to, but I cannot.

My wheelchair holds me tight.

THE BEAT

Turn on the television.

Turn on the radio.

Either one will do.

Ready for music.

Want to feel the good vibrations.

Want to sway to the beat.

Feel my hands together.

I am sure they are touching.

Feeling and hearing claps.

Bringing the right and left hands together

is difficult for me, but

I know I am clapping my hands to

the beat.

"Vibe with me."

SWEET THANG

"Miss, over there."

See me wave at you.

Trying to get your attention.

You look so fine.

Wish with all my might

you were mine.

"Yeah, you."

Hips swaying side to side.

"Can I talk to you?"

I like your bright smile.

I just want your number.

We can talk later about sweet nothings.

Let us go for a walk.

Anywhere will do.

Do you dare?

"I just want to talk to you."

I want to hear that soft voice.

Please do not turn me down.

Make me feel like a clown.

Turn my smile into a frown.

Be the talk of the town.

"Do you see the twinkle in my eyes?"

It is there for you, sweet thang.

LAUGHTER

I love to laugh.

Loud and clear.

Laugh, really laugh.

Smile, smile.

Think happy. Be happy.

Choose to be happy.

It is so inspiring.

Do happy.

A smile does change your brain's chemistry.

Think it in your mind.

I am having an adrenaline rush.

SINGING

I sing because I am happy.

I sing because you are here.

I sing because... I do not know.

All I know is that, right now,

I feel like singing.

Join me in my song?

Don't be shy.

THE HUG

I want to hug you. But you stand too far away.

"Can I hug you?" Or will you walk away?

ANY SUMMER DAY

It is a beautiful day.

The sun is out today.

Feeling excited, delighted.

Take me out into the warmth.

It is building inside me like

the intense wait for a birthday cake.

Warm rays of the sun will

stroke my face with friendly,

imaginary fingers.

The wind blows

with soft whispers of affection.

Asking with my eyes.

Asking with silent lips that quiver.

Take me outside today.

I wait patiently.

STAR JASMINE

Sweet and so fresh is the smell.

Fragrance so wonderful in the air,

floating into my nose,

transporting me

to a place of beauty.

A place of joy.

A field of flowers.

A happy grin spreads

across my face as I feel

the soft earth beneath me.

How wonderful! Star jasmine.

DESIRE

Beautiful red rose.

Draws fingers to it with desire.

Stem gives way.

Ouch!

ANOTHER DREAM

Is my life a dream?

Is this my place in the universe?

Should I be in another time?

Another place? Is this my only reality?

My only life?

"Change me, change me."

"Help me, help me."

Do not want to be here.

Like this. Why me?

Stop this nightmare.

Please, send me back to my time.

The pleasure would be all mine.

Set me free.

This is a dream, I know it.

Let me go back in time.

This is a dream.

Send me back.

TIFFANY

You remind me of a
delicate flower.
So fragile, so small, so gentle.
As giving as the sweet scent of the rose.
Remembering you.
I smile.

FLOWER IN BLOOM

Oh! Thou thorny stemmed flower blossoming in
nature's fields and gardens. Petals so perfect, so
pretty and velvet smooth to the touch. Vibrant,
deep, rich color palette of the rainbow. Perfume
fragrance envelops the scents of you who dare
come near to pick one for their pleasure. A spell is
cast upon the eyes and nose that transcends the
mind. A heavenly experience in thy presence.
The beautiful Rose.

GOODBYES

People come and go.

In and out.

Our paths cross.

Our lives are different.

Yet, the same in ways.

So soon, you are gone.

Not a word.

You disappear. Gone.

My heart touched for a moment.

Missing you now, my friend.

Your compassion.

Your kindness.

Oh! The gentle touch of your hand.

The sweet sound of your voice.

The look in your eyes that gave

peace with understanding.

People come and go.

So quickly.

So quiet, their goodbyes.

Farewell, my friend.

WHAT COLOR IS BLUE?

Blueberry jam on toast.

A smile turned upside down.

I am feeling so sad and blue.

I hurt myself.

All I see is blue sky

as I lay on the ground.

MAKE SOMEONE SMILE TODAY

Give a helping hand.

You're needed indeed.

Your perspective on life will be bright.

You will feel so good about yourself.

When you smile, the world will smile with you.

WHAT COLOR IS BLACK?

Highways stretched out as far as the eye can see.

Darkness in the night, rest in.

Sweet taste of black licorice.

Delicious Oreo cookies, "hmm mm."

Not to be outdone - dark, dark chocolate.

Please, can I have a piece?

THE LONGING

Crawling beside you.

Feeling your breath.

Hearing your sound.

Hearing your heartbeat.

Feeling your eyes on me.

Longing for your touch.

Why do you not reach for me?

WHAT COLOR IS BROWN

Sand on the beach.

Sweet light chocolate.

Tasty candy bars forever.

Honey, so sweet and good for you.

Yummy maple syrup for waffles and

pancakes. Delicious.

"Hmmmm."

WHAT COLOR IS RED?

Beating of the heart,

fast with excitement.

Ouch! Hot chili peppers.

Sweet watermelon. Red,

yellow, green, or white.

All for my delight.

Ripe strawberries.

Oh! That red.

WHAT COLOR IS PINK?

Soft, gentle touch of your fingers.

Sweet lips that plant a kiss on your

face.

Let us not forget strawberry ice cream.

Make you smile so big.

NIGHT

When the sun goes down,

blackness wraps around me and

I am peaceful.

Night beckons me to gaze up

at all the glorious stars twinkling 'hello' to me.

Colors of the stars are different

yet the same as I observe them.

Black canopy is their playground.

Stars are happy sharing their beauty

to all looking towards the heavens.

Darkness is my friend.

It takes me into dreamland as

I drift off to sleep.

Feeling so protected.

"Good night."

WHAT COLOR IS ORANGE?

Freshly squeezed oranges that produce delicious juice.

Slices of orange candy taste so good with chocolate.

Now, do not forget tangerines.

MY PAPAYA

Me, oh my, papaya candy, sweet tropical friend!

Papaya with dancing enzymes waiting to envelop my being.

Smiling, sitting at her work,

thinking of all she had accomplished today.

Fingers move with elaborate

techniques in motion. A skilled artist, for sure.

A special treat is waiting for us both.

Me, oh my, papaya!

Delicious. I know you so well.

You comfort me on good and dark days.

Effortlessly ridding my body of any discomforts.

Black seeds center my papaya, flowing through

the orange body of my papaya, delivering the strength

of vitamin "C" from Mother Earth to me.

Surging from my fingers down to my wiggly toes.

What a boost!

Full of satisfaction, ready to continue my elaborate

techniques until the day is finished.

"Yeah!"

WHAT COLOR IS WHITE?

"Look up!" The clouds are in the sky.

Billowing pillows of soft snow

on a mountain top.

Vanilla ice cream. So sweet and

delicious and satisfying.

Soft cotton bunny to hold,

snuggle with, and tickle your nose.

Nice and funny, the fluffy bunny.

WHITE LINES

Lines on the highway leading to everywhere.

Taking you to places to have fun. Places you have never seen.

Beaches to run up and down, place your feet in the cool water.

Beautiful restaurants. Delicious delicacies await you.

Eat to your heart's content. Bridges that are out of a dream.

They are for real. High as the eyes can see.

Tall buildings reaching past the clouds.

Oh! Those lines that lead me to happiness.

WHAT COLOR IS CLEAR?

Gentle winds that caress

your face, light as a whisper.

Or fierce as rain from a storm.

Water that you drink fast to

wet your dry mouth.

The breath of life.

Air.

Breathe now.

You and me.

WHAT COLOR IS YELLOW?

A lovely sunflower in a field of green.

A touch of the sun.

Sour lemons squeezed

into fresh lemonade.

Please do not

forget the sugar.

Hmm mm, so good.

In this life, if given lemons, make lemonade.

We did. The students love lemonade. When they drink, you can see their faces, twisted, eyes closed, suddenly full of smiles and sounds of laughter. Delicious.

PINEAPPLE

Delicious, sweet edible flesh, yellow as a bright sunny day, the rays touching parts of your mouth.

Zing, zing awaits you. Looks are deceiving.

The prickly spikes, 'ouch,' when managed improperly.

Touch me gently if you dare.

You will like this fleshy tropical fruit with spiked flowers (Ananas comosus). It is heavenly.

Nothing can compare to this unique fruit in the shape of a pinecone.

Sliced, diced, any way you like it. Versatility is another name, for one. Take a chance, buy one.

You will not regret it. Oh! To devour a slice of upside-down pineapple cake.

Hmmmm, to sip down a large glass of freshly squeezed pineapple juice.

Sensational as the liquid moves toward jumping taste buds.

Bingo!

Be careful how you treat angels here on earth.
They are here on a mission.

To promote love and peace. "Remember, you are
being watched by the Universe."

ENDURANCE

To endure; that is the coat we wear.

We wear it well. So well.

You do not see my tears.

Endure. Endurance

wakes me up in the morning.

Endurance taps me on my shoulder.

Endurance carries me through the day.

At night, endurance is only a memory.

Sleep, peaceful as I go

into dreamland.

Rest now, rest gives me strength.

Endure. Endurance

shall greet me in the morning.

I will greet it.

My friend.

ON THE GROUND

Slide, slide,

cannot stop.

Down I go.

Knees ache.

Legs ache.

I do not care.

It feels so good.

On bent knees.

Close to the earth.

Down here on the ground.

Sounds of laughter ring in my ear.

It is you next to me on the grass.

Down here on the ground.

In a little while, I will need your

help to get me up.

Cannot lift myself from down

here on the ground.

A CALL FOR ACTION

Feeling unloved,

feel you are outdated.

Feeling lonely,

feel you have no friends.

Feel there is something missing

in your life.

Are you trying to figure it out?

You feel a need to have influence

in the lives of others.

You can give a helping hand

to the people with disabilities.

They are waiting for you.

YOU can make a change.

Your perspective of your life will

change that day in an effective way.

Dear T.W.

To someone special who has all the virtues and senses.

You are a mentor who can turn doubt into possibility.

You are an individual who cannot be compared to others.

You always make the minutes give joy and fun.

I love to grab food from your hands and eat it like siblings do.

You have checks and balances for the cans and cannots.

You are remarkable, and you never show your sad day.

You make it troublesome to have sorrow in the heart.

Refresh me when I'm about to lose my grip and problems arise.

Sometimes, I see tears in your eyes, and you turn around with a smile.

You always present yourself with zero tribulations.

You make days worry free. Uncertainty stands alone.

On the busy days, you are always the calm individual.

I have a valuable journey with you. I hope it will last a lifetime.

I wish you and your family happiness always.

Inspiring words from one instructor to another.
Profound, beautiful words that touched my heart
and traveled to my eyes, full of tears overflowing
with gratitude. I will miss you always.

GOBBLE, GOBBLE

It is Thanksgiving.

Turkey time! "Gobble, gobble."

Goodies are being prepared in the kitchen.

Roast turkey, I can't stop looking at it.

All I can think about is that turkey.

It is glowing at me.

I can taste that turkey.

Give me some now, with golden brown stuffing.

With all the wonderful hidden treasures inside.

Topped with dripping brown gravy.

A large serving of vegetables, also mac and cheese.

Hmmm, impressive pies, apple, potato, cherry,

and pumpkin pie with marshmallows on top.

Fantastic cakes stacked three and four layers high.

Chocolate, lemon, coconut, strawberry with cream,

yellow cake with chocolate icing dripping down the sides.

A heavenly sight of deliciousness to behold.

"Gobble, gobble."

It is turkey time!

Sleep for me came early last night, expecting thanksgiving.

In the morning, delightful aromas tickle my nose

and kiss my senses to wake me,

catapulting me to my place in front of my plate

at my family's grand table.

Everyone is happy and smiling,

saying their stomachs are empty and ready to be filled.

It has been a year worth the wait for all the good
cooking.

Patience pays off.

"Gobble, gobble."

It is turkey-eating time.

Now, bow your heads.

Let us pray.

Thank God for the cook,

bless the food.

Now, let us eat.

"Gobble, gobble."

MERRY CHRISTMAS TO YOU.

"Ha! Ha! Ha! Ho! Ho! Ho!"

Listen all!

Christmas time is here, my favorite time of the year.

So near and dear to my heart.

Santa Claus is coming to my neighborhood.

I am going to see Santa Claus.

I will, I will!

Santa Claus is coming to our house, same as last year.

Santa will have his reindeer with him.

Name them if you can.

We will leave milk and cookies for

Santa Claus to support him on his way.

We do not want Santa hungry.

Santa accomplished what he came to do.

Exquisite presents under the tree for you and me.

Look! Santa left a note.

Something warm and hearty would be nice next year.

"Ha! Ha! Ha! Ho! Ho! Ho!"

"What a beautiful tree!" Santa stated.

"It is a brilliant art display of Christmas."

Bright red, yellow, blue, and green Christmas lights sparkle

and twinkle in Santa's eyes.

These dazzle and delight Santa Claus.

Waiting for Santa Claus, I am happy all day, singing Christmas songs.

Joy to the World, Peace on Earth, and more.

Can you name your favorite Christmas songs?

Sing them loud so everyone can hear you.

Santa Claus knows what I want this year.

How about you?

Have you been naughty or nice?

Remember, Santa Claus will know.

Tell the truth.

"I've been good."

"Okay."

Ha! Ha! Ha! Ho! Ho! Ho!

Merry Christmas to all!

The holidays are such a time of joy for all. It is all the students talk about for weeks. Their enthusiasm and joy lifts everyone's day and week to the highest level of pleasure and contentment. Here is another poem for Christmas time.

SANTA CLAUS TAKES A BREAK

Happy Holidays to everyone!

Christmas is so special to me.

What do I wish for every year?

Guess what? It happened.

I saw Santa Claus.

My dream came true at last.

Santa Claus was here last night.

He was in his red and white suit with his black boots fitted high.

His beard was white as snow, as shown in pictures.

He had a big smile on his face.

Santa's sled stacked high with presents,

all shapes and sizes, small and large.

Beautiful ribbons and bows wrapped them

in all the colors of the rainbow and more.

It was truly spectacular. Believe it.

Santa Claus was in my front yard with his reindeer.

You will not believe what they were doing.

They were laughing, dancing around, and playing in the snow.

They were having an enjoyable time.

Such fun was this Christmas night right there in my neighborhood, in my front yard.

Santa was singing Merry Christmas to everyone.

I watched from my window, not wanting to frighten them off.

Santa and his reindeer were taking a break

before continuing their journey

to make other people happy who

have been nice, not naughty.

I was happy it was my house they chose to stop by.

Santa looked happy waving his hands in the air.

"Time to leave," he announced.

"There are more homes to visit this night.

Breaks are wonderful, but we must move on."

Santa climbed on his sled and took the reins,

saying, "Ready" to all his reindeer.

Guess what happened next.

Santa looked right at me. Smiled big. He did, he did!

"Look under your tree!" he shouted.

"There are surprises you will see and discover."

Santa waved goodbye to me

and winked as his sled went higher and higher,

catapulting into the night sky where the stars live.

"Merry Christmas. Peace on Earth to everyone.

See you next year!" Santa said.

I heard him. I really did. I did! I ran over to our tree.

"Thank you, Santa Claus."

To you, my students; you will always be in my heart. Your laughter will ring out like a song always in my memories.

Peace and love to our true caregivers everywhere. I salute you. Humanitarians on Earth dedicated to the wellbeing of all.

To my dear friend, Bryan. Thank you for all the good times we shared with our students, the love you gave them, the adventures, and the laughter.

Thank you for your eagerness to help others and reach out, making others feel wanted.

Your bright smile. Your shy ways; wanting to live life, but afraid.

I understood you more than you understood yourself. 'Imagine' that, my friend.

FREEDOM

The butterfly emerged out of the cocoon, visible and beautiful,

from the capsule that held it prisoner. Free at last.

Metamorphosis into its destiny.

WINGS

Pain felt in the heart.

A bird with broken wings.

Now, can only tweet a sad song.

Wanting to fly into its destiny,

but unable to go from

fragrant flower to fragrant flower,

spreading love and giving seeds

of regeneration and renewal.

The need to fly is my message to you.

MY FRIEND

Friends are special people. They show up and do whatever is feasible. My friend, you had the smile of a thousand sweet, happy lips, which enhanced your prominent characteristic that lit up the world around you. Radiant and giving, always with kind words that evoked a feeling of wellbeing.

We loved you dearly without judgment, Verna V. It is our deepest hope that you felt and knew it. My friend, you did not have the chance to reach success in this place we call home, did you? Misunderstood, you suffered much. People did not understand your little quirks. Lost here, trying to sort out the problems we face every day on your tour in our world was too much for you. "Passing through," you stated. "This is not my home." Commissioned to check Earth and observe its inhabitants. Are they loving and caring for one another, showing compassion and understanding? "Earthlings, what message shall I give to the Creator?" was your question. Your journey has ended here on earth. An angel catapulted onto the wings of other angels singing, "Welcome home, little children, welcome home."

Goodbye, my friend. I will always miss you. Maybe we will meet again.

THE TRAIN

Choo, Choo!

Choo, Choo!

Hear the train whistle blowing. Far, far in the distance.

It is getting closer. It is difficult to contain my joy.

Thinking of the train, I smile with delight. I love those trains.

They call to me. Choo, Choo.

Someday, I will ride one. I will be the master.

Trains going to various parts of the country, carrying cargo of

everything you can imagine.

Did I hear moo? Maybe.

What a powerful feeling being one with the train.

Choo, choo.

Sparks flying from the metal wheels as the train

moves closer and closer to me.

The sound is riveting to my ears.

Fantastic, propelled, running at the speed of the train.

Everyone is waving from the windows to you.

Smiling and cheering you on. You try and keep up.

Feet no longer on the ground.

Taking flight. I want to go!

Swept up in a frizz of total excitement.

Catapulted into the world of the iron horse.

Imagine and believe.

Suddenly. What is this?

Movement controlled by the strings of a puppeteer.

Lifted from my bed, rubbing hands over eyes.

As I swing my feet over the side of my bed. It felt so real.

Was it? Yawn. Still not fully awake.

There it goes again. Choo, Choo.

Dreams are funny. They also come in the daytime.

ALIVE

Alive, I am, alive for sure!

No matter what happens.

Here to stay, I am.

My vibes are pure with goodness.

It is so good to feel so excited about living.

Be gone, days of woe. Got rid of the pain.

What a wonderful world I live in!

Nothing can penetrate my spirit.

Alive, I am. Look at me. Include me in.

Life has tossed me up, down, and around.

On the ground, but not out.

Now, catapulted into life, receiving all the

rewards and benefits given to humanity.

My face. Look at me smiling from ear to ear.

I am alive, yes, I am alive.

And that's a wrap.

               ∽

LIFE IS BEAUTIFUL

LIVE IT NOW TO THE FULLEST.

NO ONE KNOWS WHAT TOMORROW

WILL BRING. BE HAPPY, BE GRATEFUL.

LIVE!

               ∽

HUMANITARIAN

SAFE HAVEN

WE ABIDE YOU

OUR PROTECTOR

THE VISITOR

Buzz, buzz.

Exhausted, not sure how far I have traveled.

I need to rest.

Intense journey flying around to nowhere, but somewhere.

An open window in sight.

Steady and easy, navigating the window surrounded by vines

crawling up a brick wall from a beautiful, colorful garden below.

Protected by lush, bushy, tall green plants that are small trees.

Buzz, buzz.

Interesting.

Dare I go through this window

not knowing what I might encounter inside?

Buzz, buzz. Here it goes!

Up and down the hallway.

In one room, then another.

Finally, a safe place to land.

A comfortable spot on the wall needed at this moment.

Once landed, I will not take flight and bring attention

to this witness, looking, observing all.

Only wanting a place to regroup and fly on.

Movement gets my attention.

Who is that sitting in that chair near the fireplace?

A human being. Now quiet again.

Sudden struggling movements as though held down by an unseen force.

Whispers,

"I have miles to cross and burdens to bear.

Will I do it?

I remain on my objective to survive and thrive."

The voice a little higher, looking out into the room,

"Will someone understand my situation? After hours of observation."

Yes, this witness to all.

Just a fly on the wall.

Too small to answer your call.

Oh! How I wish I could.

Time to depart from my place on the wall.

Buzz, buzz.

Through the open window that welcomed me in.

Farewell from this fly that was a dot on the wall seeing all.

Now catapulted back into the outside world.

Oops! The birds. Buzz, buzz.

ONE PICTURE

Story is clear. Do you see what I see?

What is your interpretation

of what you see in the picture?

Tell us in a few words. Let us hear it.

Square box. Shades of gray.

Sharp corners. Closing in on you.

Fear overwhelms. Magnifying helplessness.

No escape. Wishing to walk in a quiet place.

A beautiful garden where there are fairies

flying around happily. But my life is real, it is me.

Tight feeling in chest. Creeping upward.

Forcing a reaction of warm salty water from eyes.

Flowing into a stream that has no end.

My body thinking. Sorrow and pain.

Travel on midnight train. Shall pass by soon.

Body undulates into a ball hugging knees to chest.

Rocking back and forth, as I hear

Weeping Willow weeping for me.

MODERN WESTERN AND HAIKU POEMS

Strong impressions and feelings captured in this section to tweak your imagination. Fun with the haiku world's shortest poems and modern western style poems. Both are popular.

What you capture in a moment. A picture captured in time.

Give your impressions of this photo.

Beauty in the making. Try walking.

It is great to see the world's inhabitants up close.

Days and nights, the car was my shelter and the lens for watching the activity.

Amusing, delightful, and insightful.

Seeing events that we see, but do not see.

Short stories through poetry. How beautiful and so much fun.

Poetry project finished on Valentine's Day, 2022. Coincidence maybe?

A special gift to you.

What joy to share with the world a little piece of you.

Now, it is your turn to tell your story about nature from your vantage point, your eyes, your words.

Nature Poems

Animals.

We navigate around one another day by day.

It is an admirable, but cautious relationship.

Animals are so much like us. Or are we like them?

I started writing about it recently.

Here is a little peek at my experiences.

Venture into the everyday world of our neighbors through poetry.

Haiku and modern western poems.

Short stories about nature and more.

Impressions captured in brief moments through the eyes of the author.

Having a little fun with poetry.

How about you?

Storm roars above.

Love does not cuddle with me.

Trees heavy with tears.

Bullying is tacky.

Fear, you try to engage me.

I do not stand alone.

Angry, strong, harsh winds
howling, blowing through trees,
for the sins of man.

∽

Calm is the breeze,
blowing cool air through the
weeping willow trees.

∽

Common experience
walking among redwood trees.
Sky is far away.

∽

Children run and play,
hoping the wind will blow their
misfortunes away.

∽

Thunder clouds roll by,
splash in pieces of sky.
Flowers open now.

∽

Funnel-shaped flowers,
in an array of delightful colors bloom
petals to spring. Lovely petunia.

～

Reminiscent of Mexico.
Sounds of the castanets and
Spanish flamenco dancers in
rhythm, clicking time to music.
Memories of yesterday. "Ole!"

～

Wind flows and caresses.
Gentle lilac spray.
Perfume fragrance.

～

Diminutive yellow flowers,
swaying in a field of green.
Why do you fade away?

～

In the afternoon sun,
dragonflies whisper softly
as the wind caresses.

～

Rays of energy,
piercing orange-yellow stream.
Warm morning sunrise.

Forest foliage dance.
Clear winds play music through trees.
Beautiful sound.

Waiting for spring.
Soft winter snow streams steadily.
Hibernation time.

Turkeys show feathers.
Warrior dance for battle.
Celebration now.

Morning sun beacon.
All you hear is silence.
Where are singing birds?

The little baby

bird chirps frantically.
Where are the singing birds?

White daffodils
peek through large green foliage.
Canvass moonlight sky.

Need life oxygen.
Tenuous terrestrial
bursts soil, gasping.

Caramel color.
Leaves hide cigarette butts.
Children jump in piles.

Big city lights beckon,
mesmerizing.
Delightful in beginning.
It's not home.

Testy hurricane.

Broken spirits float away,
desiring tranquil night.

Lines stretched far.
Bags float in air, silent.
Children cry hungry.

Turkeys flutter wings.
Grass is unoccupied.
No buffet dinner.

Stirs under leaves,
colorful caterpillar.
It is dinner time.

Birds peck continually,
outside on window ledge.
Spiders deprived.

Sing, sing little birds.
We warned that danger is near.

Hurrah! We are safe.

   ∽

Bird in hand priceless,
Feathers touch tree, last goodbye.
Fly away over lake.

   ∽

To soar at last.
Butterfly transformation.
Swoop, swallow, dine.

   ∽

Peck, peck. Who are you?
Another turkey imitation.
Reflection, peck.

   ∽

Leaves fall on lake.
Birds fly south, signs
winter is coming.

   ∽

In late winter months,
yellow daffodils bloom.
Hanging on for spring.

   ∽

Gazing out window.

Colored leaves dance and fall.

Vying for attention.

Jovial slumber.

Morning birds sing the sweetest songs.

Summer definite.

Straight line, forward march.

Little brown turtles find home.

Stars twinkle in sand.

Blue sky peeks through trees,

Redwoods sway, bend back and forth.

Ants march on pathway.

Gone are the snails.

The lily is now free.

Gorgeous and whole.

Tornado winds whip,

whirling spring leaves

into a frenzy.

Wind blows violently,
cascading leaves float to earth.
Soft bed underfoot.

∽

White clouds floating by.
Step in blue ocean, waves sink
In the distance, fish jumps.

∽

Hope on horizon.
Birds fly high across blue sky.
Ship in distance. "Savior."

∽

Warm sand between toes.
Ocean waves splashing on rocks.
Dreams bring tears.

∽

Hostile green landscape.
Juniper berries sprout ripe.
Hungry birds waiting.

∽

Orange, striped swirls
swimming against blue skies.
Green hills bow, sunset.

∽

Flower to flower.

Black and yellow gems.

One of nature's greatest workers.

Gift of creation.

Life is not so delicious,

without sweetness.

Love them bees.

Designer Delight.

Fashion plate, pretty.

To vogue.

Ladybug.

After gentle rain.

Each piece of clear sky.

Beauty jumps in.

OH, THOSE BIRDS!

On one special occasion of my excursions out to enjoy nature and marvel at the world around me, I had a particularly notable day. I felt very energetic and worked up an appetite. I stopped at one of my favorite spots. I felt it was too beautiful a day to eat inside. (So, takeout it was). Bag in hand, I got in my car and drove to a clear spot in the mall's parking lot. I turned off the engine, rolled down the window, put on a tune, and got ready to chow down. I do not know why, but I had the feeling someone or something was watching me. A little bird was standing near my car staring at me. "Oh! You're hungry, too. Where did you come from so quickly?" I asked while looking at the bird from my window. I added, "One should not feed animals, including you." That bird came closer to the car as if to say please. I put food in my mouth. The bird did not move. I gave in and threw a tasty fry its way. Suddenly, birds swooped in from all directions as if they had been watching, waiting all the while for that moment. I threw more food out to them. In a dash, birds gathered in a wild melee for food. These birds came close to the car. I had seen the movie "The Birds", and this reminiscence prompted me to roll up the windows. They were fighting over my food. Their racket was loud as they demanded more from me. More food was thrown to the birds out of a little crack in the window. Before I knew it, my food was all gone. My stomach growled, reminding me of my original goal. "Love those birds!" I thought.

Birds brown, blue, and black
fly from tree branch to top.
Leaves fall on cats.

～

Children play joyously,
spinning, turning cartwheels.
Summertime is here.

～

Perched on branch.
Lovebird surveys area.
Calm waiting alone.

～

Having a meeting,
high in the sky, chirping.
Birds on a wire.

～

In smog turquoise sky,
birds circle in the dark haze,
waiting on morsels.

～

Hiding in tall trees,

darting in and out of the sky.

Seeking car splats.

Oh, those birds!

Calm undercurrent

Manatee swims slowly by.

Shallow water warm.

Wall of glass.

Dark night surrounded.

Fish swim.

Home, sweet home.

TURKEYS IN ACTION

Standing, looking out my window. The day was gorgeous. Sun shining onto my face, warming my cheeks. Warming them to the touch. Feeling grateful to be a part of all this wonder. Trees green with summer's warmth. Flowers dancing in the soft breeze. Wow! How amazing is this world we live in! A big smile crosses my face.

Suddenly, there was ruckus from nearby moving in my direction. "Turkeys!" They were everywhere, showing off their feathers, bold and loud. Each male turkey walked around strutting its stuff, fanning tails with beautiful colors. A competitive display for the females. "Show-offs." Each male vying for female attention. Only the best will get a date.

Suddenly, they all stopped at the same time in front of my neighbor's shiny new car, parked in front of their house. The turkeys went wild. Pecking at the vehicle and jumping on it. My neighbors ran out to yell at the turkeys, not knowing it was their reflection on the shiny surface of the car that had set them off. As this fierce competition ceased, the turkeys sulked away, looking back with a verbal curse. People thought the turkeys did not like the car. They will learn differently when robins fly over.

Trucks, cars honk loudly.
Turkeys run across roadway.
Disappear in bush.

Why do turkeys cross the road?
Hide in bushes.
Thanksgiving is near.

LOVE FOR SURE

Love is in the air,

penetrating fortunate hearts.

Springtime is near.

    XO

Lovers reap

sunlight's warm glow from within.

Living our best life.

    OX

Son, daughter.

Love thee more.

From birth, pain

not remembered.

    XO

Life's ups and downs.

Arrow points toward heart.

Perfect gift.

    OX

Skating in winter,

as we touch in falling snow.

Cold lips become warm.

    XO

Beating hearts pump.

Red, pink, purple pedals.

Valentine's promise.

OX

Defy time, space,

getting next to you, lover.

When next we meet.

XO

Hammock sways slowly

against wind waiting, wraps

lovers in netting.

OX

Brown lips part to speak.

Lovely is the pink flower.

Delicate velvet.

XO

Sweetest is the peach

when plucked ripe from tree.

Summer memories.

OX

Hurricane in motion.

Love moves in directions.

Resistance futile.

OX

XO

Feeling trivial.

Gazing at canary sky.

Daisy held in hand.

OX

Face brushed by nature.

Lovelier by far, kissed by

true loves' lips.

XO

Wind against face.

Stars sparkling in blackest night.

Streetlight in distance.

OX

Love for sure is holding you

when your tears flow at will.

Your breathing comforts me.

XO

Love for sure is walking hand in hand

on the deck of a cruise ship,

looking at the stars.

Touch them. Maybe.

OX

Love for sure is looking into my eyes.

Saying, 'I love you,' over and over.

XO

Love for sure is playing

red light, green light

in his car.

OX

Love for sure is sheltering her from

the rain with your coat.

XO

Love for sure.

Tossing and turning,

waiting for another dream.

Sleep deprived.

XO

Night thunder roars.

Love blowing in atmosphere,

you stand before me.

OX

Exploding heart.

You love me, you love me not.

Cannot bear pain.

XO

My lover can be ever so dear.
So fabulous, touching every inch
of my existence.
What makes him so wonderful?
It is amazing how he opened the
door to my heart.

OX

Running in storm,
lightning hits violently.
Bed is uneven.

XO

Love thee so much.
Rumble, vibrate,
groove when you do.
My California.

Seasons of Life

We hear you, weeping willow.
Sitting next to you,
Troubles seem far away.
Weeping willow tree,
branches weighed down,
heavy with leaves.
Bend down and cover
bowed head and face
full of salty tears.
The forlorn consoled.
Forgery hidden.

**

Faces in the trees.
Another will emerge on
this canvas of the wind.

**

Gazing in wonder.
Looking up to thee.
Weeping willow tree,
here cometh the rain.
Tear-shaped dew forms
on leaves.

**

Calm is the breeze
blowing gently through lovely
cherry blossom trees.

**

Floral beauty open.
Lovely scent floats in air.
Delighted nostrils.

**

Orange canary.
Apples hang from tree branch.
Autumn leaves drop.

**

Standing near window.
Unexpected sound.
Raindrops on rooftop.

**

Picked up by wind,
smoke-filled leaves
blown out to sea.
Gray water reflects
on rocks.

**

Flutter rapidly.
Gentle, wind-enticed movement.
Hanging branches dance.

**

Weeping willow trees
show fluorescent colors
sparkling by moonlight

**

Wind moves branches,
swaying back and forth, waving
the mighty palm tree.

**

Green, red, yellow fruit.
Ripe tasty melon on vine,
picked in late summer.

**

Dragonflies fly freely,
spin touching blades of grass,
drinking dew gently.

**

Children run in rain,
buckets waiting to catch
pieces of gray sky.

**

Anxiously,
mountain slopes
wait to feel skies
gliding. Solid snow.

**

Frigid winter months.
All flowers and trees shiver,
waiting for summer.

**

Hurry, spring, please.
Plants thirsty for rain shower.
Reaching upwards.

**

Weeping willow tree
standing so tall,
near small pond.
Tear-soaked roots
bulldozing beneath earth
toward watery target.
Quenched thirst.

**

Note from the Author

My hope is to bolster your interest and imagination through writing of whatever may be growing inside your mind. Capturing words that stir emotions and open eyes to life. Dreams and reality can be a beautiful thing. Learning to become a master of words is an exciting adventure. Being able to condense your ideas, which showcase a point of view, is powerful.

I am learning, as well, by expressing myself with poetry, and I invite you to join my journey. This is the beginning.

Connect with me at: Wealth4rmWisdom@gmail.com

ABOUT THE AUTHOR

Terra Wilson is an avid reader who loves to venture into the world of make-believe. This fondness for imagination has inspired her to create beauty, love, and life inside *Imagine Me Over the Rainbow*.

Before publishing her debut book, *Weeping Willow, Why Are You Weeping?*, Terra worked as an assistant teacher at an elementary school which quickly became one of her first loves. Those fond memories have been deeply etched into her mind and overwhelmed with an appreciation for generous rewards from everyone, teaching didn't just become her goal, it became her career choice.

Terra is happily married and has two wonderful children.

Look around you, you will see me in smiling faces. A gentle hand assisting someone. It will be me. Be kind.

With love,

Terra Wilson